Diabetic Cooking

Healthy Diabetic Recipes to Fuel Your Body

BY: Ivy Hope

IVY HOPE
COOKBOOK

Copyright/License Page

Table of Contents

Introduction

Diabetes is a disease in which your body is unable to produce insulin or is unable to use it properly. Insulin, a hormone produced in the pancreas, is meant to control the amount of sugar (glucose) in your blood. More than eleven million Canadians and 34 million Americans are living with diabetes and dealing with its impact on their daily lives.

If you or someone you know has diabetes, then you understand how debilitating this disease can be. Chances are you have thought about what and when you are eating, and food has become a constant question for you. Even if you do not have diabetes, it can be difficult to know what foods are good and which are bad. There is a plethora of contradicting information out there, especially when it comes to proper eating with diabetes, and sifting through it can get quickly overwhelming. Websites and books differ, some will tell you that something is okay, where others say that it isn't. You may find your head spinning and you may want to simply give up from all of the confusion.

It doesn't have to be so difficult!

Living a healthy lifestyle when you suffer from diabetes means making healthy food choices and cooking meals that are rich in nutrients and low in fats. Diabetic cooking should be easy to include in your daily routine, and with this book, it can be.

The recipes in the book are created and customized for those who suffer from diabetes, but they are great for anyone who is looking to live a healthier lifestyle. The following recipes are meant to help you regulate your blood sugar while giving you the energy you need to get through the day. This book is an excellent place to start your diabetic journey and can teach you, through healthy, wholesome recipes, which foods are good for you to eat and which you should avoid.

Start your journey today and live a healthier, happier life despite diabetes.

Breakfast

Breakfast is an extremely important meal for those who are living with diabetes. A healthy breakfast will help you to feel full and satisfied, and it will create a baseline for your body's blood glucose levels. As the name states, breakfast is meant to fill the break that exists between your dinner and your lunch after you have been sleeping. When we skip breakfast, our bodies start to panic and begin to store fat to survive. Eating a healthy breakfast, however, will help to fuel your body and can even promote weight loss. People who eat breakfast tend to have healthier eating habits overall and for a diabetic, the benefits are endless. Enjoying a healthy breakfast in the morning will give you what you need to make it through the day and will regulate your blood glucose levels; helping you gain control of your diabetes. This is one meal you do not want to skip.

Very Berry Breakfast Smoothies

Prep time: 5 mins. 1 serving.

The biggest complaint people have about breakfast is not having time to eat. This terrific smoothie recipe makes breakfast fast and easy while being full of body fueling nutrients that will help you take on even the toughest days. You can whip one of these up in minutes and fuel your body on-the-go.

Ingredients:

- 1 cup non-fat yogurt
- 1 cup of frozen berries
- 1 tbsp sweet n' low or another sugar alternative
- 3 tbsp of tart juice, any flavor

How to Make Very Berry Smoothies

1. Place all ingredients into a blender and blend until smooth.

2. Pour into a glass, serve, and enjoy.

Mini, Mouthwatering Omelet Bites

Prep time: 10 mins. **Cook time:** 20 mins. 6 servings.

These small, bite-sized omelets pack a big flavor. You can make them ahead of time and store them in the fridge or freezer so you can quickly grab them on-the-go. Full of body fueling protein, these little morsels are sure to get you up.

Ingredients:

- 6 large eggs
- ½ cup low-fat milk
- ¼ cup red or green peppers
- ¼ cup cherry tomatoes, cut in half
- ½ cup shredded cheddar cheese
- 4 slices of bacon, finely chopped
- Salt and pepper

How to Make Mini, Mouthwatering Omelet Bites

1. Preheat oven to 350°

2. Cook bacon in a skillet over medium heat until crisp. Remove from heat and place on a paper towel. Leave the grease in the pan.

3. In a bowl, mix together eggs, milk, vegetables, and cheese. Add bacon and salt and pepper to the mixture and pour into greased muffin tin.

4. Bake until firm, approximately 20-25 mins.

5. Remove from oven and enjoy or store in a sealed container.

Avocado and Egg Toast

Prep time: 10 mins. 1- 2 servings.

This easy to create breakfast takes only 10 minutes to make and is packed full of powerful protein. You can create this meal in minutes and have yourself a healthy breakfast that will fill you up and fuel your body.

Ingredients:

- 2 slices of whole-grain bread
- 1 avocado, pit removed
- 1 clove of garlic, peeled
- 2 large eggs
- ¼ cup shredded cheddar cheese

How to Make Avocado and Egg Toast.

1. Toast bread to create toast.

2. In a small skillet, cook eggs until they over-easy or over-hard.

3. Rub a peeled clove of garlic on to the toast.

4. Mash avocado and spread on the toasted bread.

5. Place the cooked eggs on top of the avocado.

6. Top with shredded cheese.

7. Serve and enjoy.

Super Simple Overnight Oats

Prep time: 5 mins – plus 8-12 hours to soak. 2 servings.

Make this super simple oat recipe ahead of time for those busy weekday mornings and have a healthy breakfast in under 5 mins. This recipe is so easy to make and is sure to fill your belly. Oats are an excellent meal for diabetics and will provide you with all the fuel you need to take on the day.

Ingredients:

- 1 cup rolled oats
- 1 cup of milk
- ½ cup non-fat Greek yogurt
- 2 tbsp chia seeds
- 2 tbsp sweetener
- ½ tsp vanilla extract

*Flavor options include, peanut butter and jam, apple pie, or chocolate banana; create these by adding 1 tbsp of each of these flavors to the mixture (e.g. apple pie = diced apples + cinnamon, chocolate banana = banana + Nutella).

How to Make Super Simple Overnight Oats

1. Place all ingredients into a large glass container and stir until thoroughly combined.

2. Store covered in the refrigerator overnight.

3. Remove from the fridge and add desired toppings.

4. Enjoy.

Egg-cellent Morning Muffins

Prep time: 10 minutes. **Cook time:** 20 mins. **Total time:** 30 mins. 6 servings.

These healthy morning muffins are easy to prepare and they taste amazing. These delicious little treats can be made ahead of time and easily grabbed on the go. A great way to start the day, these morning muffins are an eggcellent source of protein.

Ingredients:

- 6 slices turkey bacon
- 2 cups egg whites
- 2 eggs
- 3 tbsp ground turkey sausage
- 1 red pepper, finely chopped
- 1 oz. spinach, finely chopped
- 1 onion, finely chopped
- 1 clove garlic, minced
- Salt and pepper

How to Make Egg-cellent Morning Muffins:

1. Preheat oven to 350°

2. Grease a muffin tin with cooking spray or margarine.

3. Wrap one slice of bacon around the inside of each muffin form

4. In a small skillet, sauté onions, peppers, and garlic for a few minutes, or until onions are translucent. Remove from heat.

5. Separate the mixture evenly between the muffin forms, adding it on top of the spinach.

6. In a bowl, mix together egg whites, eggs, salt, and pepper until well combined.

7. Pour egg mixture into muffin tins so that it covers the vegetables.

8. Bake on the middle rack for 20 minutes.

9. Serve and enjoy.

Make Now, Eat Later Breakfast Bowls

Prep time: 10 minutes. **Cook time:** 20 mins. **Total time:** 30 mins. 6 servings

These delicious breakfast bowls are super simple to make and always taste amazing. You make them ahead of time and heat them later, allowing the flavors to settle and a mouthwatering meal to brew. This dish is super healthy and filling, and it will give you all the energy you need to take on the day.

Ingredients:

- 1 onion, finely chopped
- 8 large eggs
- 1 lb. potatoes, cut into cubes
- ½ cup cheddar cheese, shredded
- 1 each red and green peppers, finely chopped
- Salt and Pepper
- Olive oil

How to Make Breakfast Bowls:

1. Preheat oven to 425°

2. Add potatoes, peppers, and onions to a large baking pan drizzled with olive oil.

3. Season with salt and pepper and toss to coat.

4. Bake for 25-35 minutes, until potatoes are golden brown; flipping halfway through.

5. Crack eggs into a bowl while the vegetables are cooking and whisk until smooth. Season with salt and pepper.

6. Warm a large skillet over medium heat that has been sprayed with cooking spray. Cook eggs until they are almost ready but still slightly glossy. Set aside.

7. Scoop potatoes and eggs into containers and toss to combine. Allow the mixture to cool completely.

8. Sprinkle with cheese and store in the refrigerator for 3 days or freeze for later.

9. Enjoy.

Make Now, Eat Later Breakfast Berry Parfait

Prep time: 5 mins 2 Servings.

The perfect little parfaits make an excellent breakfast. They are packed full of good-for-you foods that will give you all the energy you need to start the day. Delicious nuts, healthy seeds, and some fresh fruits make this a meal that is sure to fuel you.

Ingredients:

- 12 oz. Greek yogurt
- ½ cup old fashioned oats, raw
- 2 tbsp. chia seeds
- ¼ cup milk
- 2 cups frozen mixed berries

How to Make Breakfast Berry Parfaits:

1. Mix together yogurt and oats. Add chia seeds and milk and mix well. Layer half the mixture inside a container and add frozen berries. Add the remaining yogurt mixture on top of the berries and refrigerate overnight.

2. Enjoy.

Healthy Whole Wheat Waffles

Prep time: 25 mins. 24 waffles.

Waffles are an easy breakfast that the whole family will enjoy. You can make these whole wheat waffles ahead of time and store them in the freezer for up to 3 months. They are a super simple, grab-and-go meal that works perfectly for busy weekday mornings. Just pull them out of the freezer, pop them into the toaster and you have a healthy meal in minutes.

Ingredients:

- 4 large eggs
- 3 cups of milk
- ¼ cup maple syrup
- ¼ cup butter or oil
- 2 tbsp. vanilla extract
- 1 tsp. baking powder
- ½ - 1 tsp. sea salt
- 4 cups whole wheat flour

How to Make Healthy Whole Wheat Waffles:

1. In a large bowl, beat the eggs until smooth. Mix in milk, vanilla, oil, maple syrup, baking powder, and salt; whisk to fully combine.

2. Add whole wheat flour and mix well.

3. Heat the waffle maker and spray with cooking spray if needed.

4. Cook waffles according to appliance instructions.

5. *Note: The amount of batter used will depend on the size of the waffle maker but usually you will use approximately 1/3 cup per waffle.

6. Store in the fridge for up to a week or freeze for up to 6 months in an airtight container.

7. Top with syrup, fresh fruit, or whipped topping to serve.

8. Enjoy.

Healthy Whole Wheat Pancakes

Prep time: 20 mins. 10-12 pancakes.

These healthy pancakes are sure to become a family favorite. Perfect for those lazy weekend mornings, this recipe uses simple ingredients to create a meal you are guaranteed to enjoy. The soft, fluffy texture and dreamy buttermilk flavor will hit the spot and fill you up so that you can tackle the day ahead. The use of whole wheat flour makes these pancakes both delicious and healthy, and the fresh fruit toppings take this recipe over the top.

Ingredients:

- 2 cups of milk
- ½ cup white vinegar
- 3 to 4large eggs
- ½ cup oil
- ½ cup maple syrup
- 1 ½ tsp baking powder
- 1 ½ tsp baking soda
- ½ tsp salt
- 3 to 3 ½ cups whole wheat flour

How to Make Healthy Whole Wheat Pancakes:

1. In a bowl, mix together milk and vinegar. Let stand 7-10 mins. The mixture will curdle and thicken to create buttermilk.

2. Add eggs, oil, maple syrup, baking soda, baking powder, and salt to the buttermilk mixture and stir to combine.

3. Add the flour, mixing gently to combine. Ensure there are no clumps or dry chunks.

4. Preheat skillet with a small amount of oil.

5. Spread batter in a circular shape on the skillet and cook for 3-4 minutes per side. Repeat with all the remaining batter, placing the finished pancakes on a plate when done.

6. Top with butter, syrup, and fresh fruit.

7. Enjoy.

Lunch

The timing of meals plays a key role in managing diabetes. You do not have to eat at specific times each day, but you should be eating regularly. Like breakfast, which breaks up the fasting between dinner and lunch; lunch is meant to break up the afternoon and fuel your body for the remaining part of the day. If you have ever hit that afternoon slump, you know the importance of a good, healthy lunch to get you through until dinner. The great news is there are so many quick and healthy options available out there. You can easily create a healthy lunch that you are sure to love, and one that will give you all the vitamins you need to tackle those busy afternoons.

Thick and Creamy Split Pea Soup

Prep time: 15 mins. **Total time:** 5 hours. 4 servings.

This fantastic family favorite is so filling and amazingly delicious. Great for cold winter afternoons, this meal is sure to fill your belly and give you all the energy you need for the rest of the day. With only 15 minutes to prepare, you can walk away and come back to an excellent lunch that you are guaranteed to love.

Ingredients:

- 2 cups of ham, cubed
- 1 cup green split peas, dried
- 1 rib of celery, finely chopped
- 1 carrot, finely chopped
- 1 small onion, finely chopped
- 3 cups of water
- 1 bottle of light beer
- ½ tbsp. English mustard
- ½ cup milk, 2%
- 1 tbsp. parsley, minced
- Salt and pepper
- Pinch of nutmeg

How to Make Thick and Creamy Split Pea Soup:

1. Place ham, peas, celery, carrot, and onion in the slow cooker. Add water, beer, and mustard.

2. Cook on high for 5 hours, until peas are tender.

3. Remove from slow cooker, top with parsley, and enjoy!

Easy and Delicious Grown-up Chicken Nuggets

Prep time: 30 mins. 4 servings.

These delicious little morsels are so easy to make and they tasted amazing. Eat them on their own or place them in a wrap with mayo or ranch. No matter how you choose to eat these little treats, you are sure to be satisfied.

Ingredients

- ½ cup all-purpose flour
- 2 tsp. Le Grille brand seasoned salt
- ½ tsp. poultry seasoning
- ½ tsp. ground mustard
- ½ tsp. paprika
- Pinch of pepper
- 1 lb. boneless skinless chicken breast
- 2 tbsp. oil

How to Make Grown-up Chicken Nuggets:

1. In a shallow dish, combine the dry ingredients.

2. Flatten or cut the chicken into half-inch-thick pieces and into small bite-sized chunks.

3. Coat chicken with dried spices by gently tossing and flipping in the mixture.

4. Cook chicken in a large skillet covered in oil until no longer pink, approximately 6-8 minutes.

5. Serve and enjoy.

Terrific Tuna Sandwich

Prep time: 20 mins. 2 Servings.

Tuna is an excellent lunch option. It is full of good-for-you nutrients and is easy and affordable. This tuna sandwich is packed full of protein that will fuel your body and have you ready to take on anything. You can put this tuna sandwich together quickly and eat a healthy, flavorful lunch that you will love.

Ingredients:

- 1 can of tuna, drained and flaked
- 1 hardboiled egg, finely chopped
- 1 cup mayonnaise
- ½ small onion, finely chopped or grated
- 1 tsp. parsley
- ¼ tsp onion powder
- 1 pinch garlic powder
- 4 slices whole-wheat toast
- ½ cup cheddar cheese, shredded

How to Make Terrific Tuna Sandwiches

1. Preheat the oven to 425° or heat a toaster oven.

2. Combine all ingredients except the bread and cheese.

3. Place mixture on to of each slice of bread and top with grated cheese.

4. Toast for 1-2 minutes or until cheese is melted and bread is toasted.

5. Serve open-faced or as a sandwich.

6. Enjoy.

The Best Blue Cheese Buffalo Chicken Lettuce Wraps

Prep time: 20 mins. 2 servings.

These spicy and flavorful little wraps are sure to delight your tastebuds. The kick of hot sauce and cool creaminess of the blue cheese combine to make a fabulous flavor that you are sure to enjoy. So easy to make, you can whip these up and pack them for lunch any day of the week.

Ingredients:

- ½ lb. ground chicken
- 1 stalk of celery, finely chopped
- 1 pinch of pepper
- 2 tbsp ketchup
- 2 tbsp. hot sauce
- 1 ½ tbsp. brown sugar
- 1 tbsp. mustard
- 6 lettuce leaves
- ½ tbsp apple cider vinegar
- Crumbled blue cheese for topping

How to Make the Best Blue Cheese Buffalo Chicken Wraps:

1. In a large skillet, cook chicken over medium heat, crumbling as it cooks.

2. Stir in celery and pepper, cooking until no longer pink; approximately 2-3 minutes.

3. Add ketchup, hot sauce, brown sugar, mustard, and vinegar. Bring to a boil.

4. Reduce heat and simmer for 5 minutes, stirring occasionally.

5. Serve in lettuce leaves topped with blue cheese.

6. Enjoy.

Oh-So-Good Egg Salad

Prep time: 20 mins. 2 servings.

Egg salad, like tuna, is full of protein, is affordable, and is so easy to prepare. This egg salad recipe steps it up with a kick of mustard that brings out the flavors in this sandwich. Make this egg salad ahead of time and enjoy it later or eat it immediately. It can be created in minutes and give you all the fuel you need to be a boss in that afternoon meeting.

Ingredients:

- 4 large eggs
- ¼ cup mayonnaise
- ½ tsp. yellow mustard
- 2 tbsp. finely chopped onion
- Salt and Pepper
- Pinch of paprika

How to Make Oh-So-Good Egg Salad:

1. Hard boil eggs by boiling for 10 minutes.

2. Remove from water, cool, and peel. Chop eggs into small bits and place them in a bowl.

3. Mix mayonnaise, mustard, and onion with the chopped eggs.

4. Season with salt, pepper, and paprika.

5. Create a sandwich or wrap and enjoy.

The Queen of Cucumber Salad

Prep time: 20 min. Serves 4.

This terrific cucumber salad is packed with protein in the form of chickpeas. Creamy feta cheese and a pinch of spices make this a delicious meal you won't soon forget. Marinate the chickpeas overnight for a fabulous, flavorful lunch you are guaranteed to love. Just be careful, your coworkers may steal this one from under your nose.

Ingredients:

- 1 small (8 oz) can of chickpeas
- ½ tbsp balsamic vinegar
- 1 ½ tsp extra virgin olive oil
- Pinch of seasoning blend
- 1 cup diced tomatoes
- 1 cup diced cucumbers, unpeeled
- ¼ cup parsley or oregano, finely chopped
- ¼ cup feta, crumbled
- Salt and pepper

How to Make the Queen of Cucumber Salad:

1. Rinse chickpeas well and dry with a paper towel.

2. Combine olive oil, vinegar, and seasoning spice and whisk.

3. Pour oil dressing mixture over the chickpeas and marinate in the refrigerator overnight to enhance flavor (if possible).

4. Once you are ready to create the salad, remove beans from the fridge and drain them, setting the dressing aside. *If you need more dressing, add a bit more oil and vinegar.

5. Dice tomatoes and cucumbers so that you have small, bite-sized pieces.

6. Combine tomatoes and cucumbers with the chickpeas and toss in the dressing.

7. Season with salt and pepper, and gently mix in the feta cheese.

8. Serve and enjoy.

Amazing Avocado and Zucchini Soup.

Prep time: 10 minutes. Serves 4.

This incredible avocado and zucchini soup is the perfect lunch option. It is full of good-for-you nutrients and is served cold. Whip this up in minutes and pack it in your bag for a delicious lunch at the office. Perfect for hot summer days, this chilled soup is quick and easy to create and so delicious.

Ingredients:

- 1 leek, cleaned and finely chopped
- ½ tbsp extra virgin olive oil
- 1 zucchini, finely chopped
- 1 cucumber, chopped
- ¼ cup cilantro
- 2 Tbsp scallions, finely chopped
- Pinch of ground cumin
- ¼ cup of coconut milk
- ½ cup of water
- 1 avocado
- Salt and pepper

How to Make Amazing Avocado and Zucchini Soup.

1. Heat oil in a small skillet.

2. Add leeks and sauté until soft, approximately 4 minutes.

3. Place leeks into the blender with all other ingredients and blend until smooth.

4. Chill in the fridge or serve immediately.

5. Enjoy.

Dinner

While every meal that diabetic eats is important, dinner is essential to controlling diabetes. Dinner provides your body with the nutrients it needs to get through the night. As a diabetic, you should be eating regularly throughout the day to maintain your glucose levels. Dinner is the last big meal of the day and provides your body with the fuel it needs to rest through the night. Although you can have a snack later in the evening, eating a healthy dinner will help you resist eating snacks that are unhealthy or dangerous for this disease. Be sure to have a healthy, filling dinner so that your body has all the nutrition it needs for the night.

Avocado Orange Skillet Salmon

Prep time: 20 mins. 4 Servings.

Salmon is one of the best types of fish. It is full of flavor and so good for you. This amazing recipe uses avocados and oranges to create a tasty salsa for this fish that is fresh and crisp. The sweet, smoky flavors of this meal are sure to delight your taste buds and fill your belly. This is a quick and healthy meal that your whole family will love.

Ingredients:

- 4 salmon fillets
- 2 ½ tbsp. maple syrup
- 2 oranges, peeled and sectioned
- ½ tsp. orange rinds
- ½ tbsp. Cointreau
- 1 avocado, peeled and diced
- Juice from ½ an orange
- 1 tbsp. red onion, finely chopped
- 1 tbsp. red and green pepper, finely chopped
- ½ tbsp. chives, finely chopped
- ½ tbsp lime juice
- Salt and pepper

How to Make Avocado Orange Skillet Salmon:

1. Heat a skillet over medium heat.

2. In a small saucepan, add together maple syrup, Cointreau, and orange rinds, bring to a boil and cook for 3 minutes. Let cool.

3. Add a small pinch of salt and pepper to the fish and brush with the syrup mixture.

4. Place fish onto skillet and grill for 8-12 minutes or until the fish easily flakes.

5. Combine a pinch of salt and pepper, avocado, orange sections, juices, onion, peppers, and chives in a medium bowl for serving with the fish.

6. Serve over rice or crusty bread.

7. Enjoy.

Creamy Grilled Fajitas with Avocado Mash

Prep time: 20 mins. 4 Servings.

These amazing fajitas are full of flavor and so easy to make. The creamy, yogurt sauce is made rich with garlic and spices but adds a creamy flavor your whole family will love. The spice of jalapenos and the depth of the smoked paprika make this meal an exotic option you will want to make again and again. So quick and flavorful, this is sure to become a weeknight favorite that everyone will enjoy.

Ingredients:

- 3 cloves of garlic, minced
- 1 cup plain yogurt
- 1 tsp. smoked paprika
- ½ tsp. ground cumin
- ½ tsp. coriander, ground
- ½ tsp oregano
- 4 small chicken breasts
- 3 tomatoes, finely chopped
- 1 small onion, finely chopped
- 1 each red and green peppers, finely chopped
- 1 jalapeno, finely chopped
- ½ cup finely chopped fresh coriander
- Juice of 1 lime
- 4 tortillas
- 2 avocados, cut in have and mashed

How to make Creamy Grilled Fajitas with Avocado Mash

1. Mix together garlic and yogurt. Spoon into a small bowl and add spices and oregano, stir well.

2. Toss chicken in the mixture until fully coated.

3. Heat a skillet with a small amount of oil and cook the chicken and peppers for 5 minutes, or until fully cooked but still moist.

4. Mix together tomatoes, onion, jalapeno, coriander, and lime.

5. Heat tortillas and spoon fresh avocado onto the tortilla and spread evenly. Add the chicken and the salsa you created and add a spoonful of garlic yogurt mixture on top.

6. Serve while hot and enjoy.

Spectacular Stuffed Peppers

Prep time: 30 mins. 4 Servings.

This super-easy vegetarian meal is bursting with fun flavors that your whole family will love. These peppers are easy to make and taste delicious. Once you try them, you will never make stuffed peppers any other way.

Ingredients:

- 1 cup couscous, rinsed and drained
- ¼ cup raisins
- 2 tbsp parsley, finely chopped
- 2 tbsp pine nuts
- 1 cup crumbled feta cheese
- Pinch of cinnamon
- ¼ cup olive oil
- 4 red peppers, tops cut and insides scraped

How to make Spectacular Stuffed Peppers:

1. Heat oven to 350°

2. Place couscous and raisins in a glass bowl and cover with boiling water. Let stand for 5-8 minutes.

3. Using a fork, fluff the couscous and stir in the parsley, pine nuts, half the feta, cinnamon, and half the oil. Mix thoroughly.

4. Stuff the peppers with the mixture and set them in a roasting pan. Top with the remaining feta cheese and drizzle with oil.

5. Bake in the oven for 15-17 minutes, or until feta is baked and golden.

6. Serve and enjoy.

Comforting Cauliflower Mac 'n Cheese

Prep time: 30 mins. 6-8 Servings.

Two classic comfort foods combine to make this amazing family meal. The creamy flavor and abundance of cheese are sure to make this one of your go-to comfort foods in the future. A meal the whole family is sure to love, they will be begging for seconds and asking you to make this dish every day.

Ingredients:

- 1 ½ cups macaroni noodles
- 1 head of cauliflower, cut into small pieces
- ¼ cup butter
- ¼ cup flour
- 4 cups of milk
- 1 cup grated old cheddar cheese
- 3 cloves of garlic, minced
- ¼ cup breadcrumbs
- 1 tsp thyme, finely chopped

How to Make Comforting Cauliflower Mac 'n Cheese

1. Bring a pot of salted water to a boil and cook pasta for 5 minutes. Add in the cauliflower and continue boiling for an additional 10 minutes. Drain and reserve a small amount of the cooking water.

2. Melt butter in a pan over low heat.

3. Stir in flour and slowly pour in the milk, being careful to stir constantly until sauce thickens. Allow sauce to gently boil for a few moments before removing from the heat. Add sauce to the cooking water and season to taste.

4. Pour cauliflower and pasta into a large casserole dish. Stir to combine pasta, cauliflower, and sauce completely.

5. Thoroughly mix the garlic, thyme, and breadcrumbs and sprinkle over the top of the casserole dish and top with more grated cheese. Bake for 3-4 minutes, or until the dish is bubbling.

6. Serve and enjoy.

Super Easy Sausage Meatballs and Rice

Prep time: 20 mins. Serves 4.

This recipe is my go-to on the busy days when I don't feel like cooking. You can whip this meal up in no time and your family will gobble it up. You create meatballs out of whole sausages by cutting them into chunks and cook them up in sweet tomato sauce. Add a few peppers and other veggies and you are done. It is so easy and so delicious that you will want to make it all the time.

Ingredients:

- 6-8 mild Italian sausages
- 2 cans garlic and basil flavor tomato sauce
- 1 each red, green, and yellow peppers, chopped into small pieces
- 1 small onion, finely chopped
- 2 cloves of garlic, minced
- 1 small jar of salsa, medium
- ½ cup grated cheddar cheese
- 2 cups cooked rice

How to make Super Easy Sausage Meatballs and Rice:

1. Remove sausages from casing and roll into small meatballs, ensuring consistent size.

2. In a large skillet, cook sausage meatballs over medium-high, turning and rolling as they cook.

3. Add peppers and garlic to the skillet and fry with meatballs for 5 minutes.

4. Pour the tomato sauce, and salsa into the skillet with the other ingredients and reduce heat to low. Allow mixture to simmer for 5-10 minutes. Meanwhile, cook rice, adding it to the skillet, and stirring to blend once cooked.

5. Spoon into bowls and top with grated cheese.

6. Serve and enjoy.

Vegetarian Sheppard's Pie

Prep time: 45 mins. 6 servings.

One taste of this terrific vegetarian shepherd's pie will have you longing for more. This recipe is packed full of fantastic vegetables and meets all the standard intake requirements. It is both healthy and delicious. Your family is guaranteed to gobble it up and search for seconds.

Ingredients:

- 2 ½ tbsp olive oil
- 2 onions, sliced or finely chopped
- 1 /2 tbsp. flour
- 1 ½ cups carrots, chopped into small pieces
- 1 cauliflower, cut into small pieces
- 4 cloves of garlic, minced
- 1 tsp. rosemary, finely chopped
- 1 large can of diced tomatoes
- 1 cup each of frozen peas and corn
- 3 cups of potatoes, cut into chunks
- ½ to 1 cup of milk
- ½ to 1 cup of shredded cheddar cheese

How to Make Vegetarian Sheppard's Pie:

1. Heat 1 tbsp of oil in a skillet over medium heat and add onions, cook for 8-10 minutes, or until soft.

2. Stir in the flour and cook for another 2 mins.

3. Add in the garlic, rosemary, carrots, and cauliflower; cook for 5 minutes.

4. Pour the tomatoes into the skillet with a full can of water, stir to combine.

5. Cover with a lid and simmer for 12 minutes, stirring occasionally.

6. Remove lid and cook for 15 mins, until sauce thickens.

7. Stir in the peas and cook for another 2 mins.

8. Meanwhile, boil the potatoes for 15 minutes, until they are nice and tender. Mash the cooked potatoes with milk and add the remaining oil and season to taste.

9. Place the oven on broil and spoon the vegetable mixture into a pie dish. Top with mashed potatoes, dragging fork to create markings.

10. Heat the pie tin for 3-5 minutes, or until the top is crisp and golden.

11. Add shredded cheese on top and broil for 1 more minute.

12. Serve and enjoy.

Simple Baked Chicken Breast

Prep time: 35 mins. 4 servings.

This baked chicken breast recipe is so easy to create and comes out so juicy every single time. The prep takes mere minutes, and it is simple to throw together. This recipe is absolutely delicious, and it is sure to become your go-to meal for busy weeknights.

Ingredients:

- 4 large chicken breasts, boneless and skinless
- ½ tbsp. avocado oil
- ½ tsp. smoked paprika
- ½ tsp. garlic powder
- ½ tsp. oregano
- Pinch of each salt and pepper

How to Make Simple Baked Chicken Breast:

1. Preheat the oven to 450°

2. Drizzle chicken with oil and sprinkle with paprika. Add garlic, oregano, salt, and pepper then place in a large baking dish ensuring all sides are evenly coated.

3. Bake for 25-30 minutes.

4. Serve with a fresh salad and enjoy.

Sweet Potato Skillet

Prep time: 30-40 mins. 4 servings.

This quick and easy sweet potato skillet meal takes 30 minutes to make and is full of flavor. The healthy mixture of sweet potatoes, beans, corn, and grated cheese blend together to create a meal the whole family will enjoy. Fresh lime juice adds a crisp flavor you will not soon forget. This meal can be made in no time and is perfect for any day of the week.

Ingredients:

- 1 lb. sweet potatoes, cut into small cubes
- 1 onion, finely chopped
- 1 to 2 cloves of garlic, minced
- 1 tbsp oil, coconut, avocado, or olive
- 1 large red pepper, diced into small pieces
- 1 can of black beans, drained
- ½ cup of frozen corn
- 1 can diced tomatoes
- ½ tbsp cumin
- ¼ tbsp. taco seasoning
- Pinch of salt
- ½ lime, juiced
- 1 cup shredded cheddar cheese, Tex Mex or Old Cheddar
- 1 large avocado, diced
- 2 tsp. cilantro, finely chopped
- Salsa and Greek yogurt for serving

How to Make Sweet Potato Skillet:

1. Heat a large, deep skillet coated with oil.

2. Add sweet potatoes, cumin, and salt; cook for 5 minutes. Stir occasionally.

3. Mix in the onion, garlic, and bell pepper; cook for another 3 minutes.

4. Add the beans, corn, and tomatoes, along with the taco seasoning and pepper. Stir and bring to a boil. Reduce heat to low and simmer for 12-15 mins.

5. Turn off the burner and stir in the avocado, cilantro, and lime.

6. Sprinkle cheese over the mixture and cover to allow the cheese to melt.

7. Serve with Greek yogurt and salsa.

8. Enjoy.

Snacks

When you have diabetes, snacking can be a scary thing. What can you eat? What can you not eat? How much can you eat? When should you eat? There is an ample amount of conflicting evidence out there when it comes to the right foods for people with diabetes and it can become very overwhelming. A good rule of thumb to follow is to choose healthy foods and eat small portion sizes frequently throughout the day. Eggs, whole grains, and vegetables are always good choices and can provide you with the nutrients you need to make it through the day. The most important thing is to have healthy options on hand that you can eat when you are hungry. This will help you avoid grabbing whatever is convenient as most store-bought snacks are full of sugar. Snacking may be confusing, but it does not have to be. There are many excellent snack ideas for you to choose from and enjoy.

Mini Frittatas

Prep time: 25 mins. 12 servings.

Mini Frittatas make an excellent snack. These small bites are packed full of protein and can be made to suit any flavor craving you might have. Make them ahead of time and eat them later or pack them as a snack at the office. These great treats are a good grab-and-go option for when hunger strikes.

Ingredients:

- 10 paper muffin liners
- ½ cup onions, finely chopped
- 6 eggs
- 4 egg whites
- Salt and pepper
- Cheddar cheese, grated

How to Make Mini Frittatas:

1. Preheat oven to 375°

2. Line muffin tins with paper liners.

3. Heat a skillet with cooking spray over medium heat. Add onions and peppers to the skillet and cook for 4-5 minutes.

4. Remove from heat.

5. In a bowl, mix together the eggs, cheese, onions, and peppers until fully blended.

6. Pour the mixture into muffin cups that are lined with paper and bake for 20 mins.

7. Serve and enjoy.

Roasted Chickpeas

Prep time: 45 mins. 8 servings.

This fantastic snack is full of fiber and a much better choice than potato chips. Full of flavor, these tiny treats pack the perfect amount of crunch. You can make a large batch and store them for snacks that are easy to grab when you are hungry.

Ingredients:

- 2 cans chickpeas or garbanzo beans, drained
- Pinch of salt
- Pinch of garlic salt
- Pinch of cayenne pepper
- 4 tbsp olive oil

How to Make Roasted Chickpeas:

1. Preheat oven to 450°

2. Drain chickpeas and dry lightly with a paper towel.

3. In a bowl, toss chickpeas in olive oil and season with salt, garlic salt, and cayenne pepper.

4. Spread evenly over a baking sheet and bake for 35-40 minutes.

5. Serve and enjoy or store in an airtight container for later.

Terrifically Tangy Tuna Salad

Prep time: 10 mins. 2 servings.

Tuna salad makes for an excellent, protein-filled snack. This tangy version of this ultimate classic uses mustard and relish to add a slight surprise of flavor that you are sure to love. Use bell peppers instead of bread to eat this delicious treat and you are guaranteed to enjoy the satisfying crunch it will provide. Perfect for snacking in mid-day, this recipe will provide you with all the fuel you need for the day ahead.

Ingredients:

- 1 can of tuna, drained
- ¼ cup carrot, finely chopped
- ¼ cup celery, finely chopped
- ¼ cup mayonnaise
- 2 tsp. honey mustard
- 1 tsp. sweet relish
- Salt and pepper
- 6 large bell peppers, cut into large chunks

How to Make Tangy Tuna Salad:

1. Mix all ingredients together well.

2. Use chopped peppers to scoop the tuna.

3. Enjoy.

Fresh Fruit Kebabs

Prep time: 15 mins. 6 servings.

These fresh fruit kebabs are a healthy option for the whole family. Kids love these little skewers because they make fruit fun to eat. The variety of fruits provide a crisp and refreshing snack that is packed full of nutrients.

Ingredients:

- 6 cups of watermelon, cut into chunks
- 6 cups of pineapple, cut into chunks,
- 6 cups of cantaloupe, cut into chunks
- 2 mangos, cut into bite-size pieces
- 6 blackberries
- 6 strawberries, halved
- 2 kiwis, sliced and halved

*Serve with yogurt or whipped topping.

How to Make Fresh Fruit Kebabs:

1. Thread chopped up fruit onto wooden skewers.

2. Place on serving tray or plate with yogurt or whipped topping for dipping.

3. Serve and enjoy it.

Salty and Sweet Coconut Chips

Prep time: 15-18 mins. 4 servings.

When you crave something sweet or salty snacking can be difficult. Often times we reach for potato chips or chocolate to solve our cravings and these snacks are full of sugar and other bad things. Instead of those options, try these terrific coconut chips. The sweet and salty flavors are sure to satisfy all your cravings and will have you searching for more. You can make these ahead of time and store them for later or enjoy them immediately. Kids will love these little slices of heaven and they are so much better for you than a bag of chips. So easy to make, this delicious snack uses only 3 ingredients but is so tasty.

Ingredients:

- 2 tbsp coconut oil
- 1 ½ coconut flakes
- 4 g sea salt

How to Make Salty and Sweet Coconut Chips:

1. Preheat oven to 300°

2. Melt coconut oil in skillet or jelly roll pan.

3. Mix coconut and sea salt into the coconut oil.

4. Bake for 7-9 mins, watching carefully until they are golden brown.

5. Drain and blot using a paper towel.

6. Serve and enjoy.

Amazing Burger Bowls

Prep time: 25 mins. 2 servings.

These delicious burger bowels are so filling and fun. Both kids and adults will gobble these up and ask for seconds. Quick to throw together, this makes the perfect mid-week meal. This recipe is great because you can easily adjust the size and you can add anything you like, and it will still taste amazing. When you want something that is fast and filling, this will become your go-to meal.

Ingredients:

- 1 ½ tbsp. milk
- 1 tbsp quick-cooking oats
- Pinch of salt, cumin, chili powder, and pepper
- ½ lb. lean ground turkey or chicken
- 2 cups baby kale
- 1 cup fresh pineapple cut into small pieces
- 1 mango, peeled and sliced thin
- 1 avocado, peeled and sliced
- 1 red pepper, cut into thin strips
- 2 tomatoes, sliced thin
- ¼ cup chipotle mayo

How to Make Amazing Burger Bowls:

1. In a large bowl, mix milk, turkey, oats, and seasoning.

2. Create 2 burger patties with your hands.

3. Place burgers on an oiled skillet or grill and cook for 4-5 minutes per side.

4. Serve with salad and enjoy.

Conclusion

For those that suffer from diabetes, eating can cause a great deal of stress. Wondering what to eat and when to eat, it can quickly take over your life. There is a plethora of misinformation out there that can cause confusion and leave you feeling overwhelmed. It is important that you remember having diabetes simply means making healthier choices and eating regularly throughout the day. The recipes in this book are designed to inspire your inner chef. There are great ideas from breakfast to dinner that are healthy and fast to make. There are grab and go options as well if you pre-plan.

Diabetes can be overwhelming, but it does not have to be. Use the recipes in this book to guide and inspire you to live the best possible life despite this disease and enjoy all the amazing foods that life has to offer.

About the Author

Ivy's mission is to share her recipes with the world. Even though she is not a professional cook she has always had that flair toward cooking. Her hands create magic. She can make even the simplest recipe tastes superb. Everyone who has tried her food has astounding their compliments was what made her think about writing recipes.

She wanted everyone to have a taste of her creations aside from close family and friends. So, deciding to write recipes was her winning decision. She isn't interested in popularity, but how many people have her recipes reached and touched people. Each recipe in her cookbooks is special and has a special meaning in her life. This means that each recipe is created with attention and love. Every ingredient carefully picked, every combination tried and tested.

Her mission started on her birthday about 9 years ago, when her guests couldn't stop prizing the food on the table. The next thing she did was organizing an event where chefs from restaurants were tasting her recipes. This event gave her the courage to start spreading her recipes.

She has written many cookbooks and she is still working on more. There is no end in the art of cooking; all you need is inspiration, love, and dedication.

Author's Afterthoughts

I am thankful for downloading this book and taking the time to read it. I know that you have learned a lot and you had a great time reading it. Writing books is the best way to share the skills I have with your and the best tips too.

I know that there are many books and choosing my book is amazing. I am thankful that you stopped and took time to decide. You made a great decision and I am sure that you enjoyed it.

I will be even happier if you provide honest feedback about my book. Feedbacks helped by growing and they still do. They help me to choose better content and new ideas. So, maybe your feedback can trigger an idea for my next book.

Thank you again

Sincerely

Ivy Hope